U0912834

THE WORLD OF CHINESE MAGAZINE
《汉语世界》杂志社编

CULTURAL FILES

+ CULTURAL RELICS

中国文化档案：人文景观

商務印書館 The Commercial Press
SINCE 1897
2011, Beijing

Publisher: Yu Dianli

Production Supervisor: Zhou Hongbo

Mastermind / Chief Editor: Cao Quan

Art director / Designer: Yuke Wang

Executive Editors: Wen Xuechun, He Hongtao, Zhao Lei

Proofreaders: Yu Libin, Zhao Yuhong

Special thanks to:

China Great Wall Society, The Huangchengxiangfu Group,
Shaolin Monastery, Zhu Xiaojian, H. R. Lan (USA), David N. Tool (USA),
Li Bing, Cui Yonghua, Andy Deemer (USA), Jonathan Heeter (USA),
Robert Lewis Livingston (USA), Nicholas Richards (Canada),
Tian Wenzhu, Zhao Zhankun, Ma Shirui

CHAPTERS

THE STORY OF THE GREAT WALL 02

1. Walls of Earlier Dynasties
2. The Ming Great Wall
3. Why It Was Built
4. Cultural Symbol and World Heritage
5. Legends of the Great Wall

SHAOLIN MONASTERY TODAY 26

1. Approaching Shaolin Monastery
2. The Source of Kung Fu
3. Shaolin Culture Goes Global
4. A Monk's Life

MYSTERY OF THE MOUNTAIN MANSION 54

1. What Is the Royal Residence of the Premier?
2. Castle or House?
3. The Birthplace of *The Kangxi Dictionary*
4. Historic Huangcheng Village

HEAVENLY HUIZHOU 78

1. Black Tiles and White Walls
2. Fortunes Spent
3. Memorial Arch: A Stone Award
4. Living History Along the Ancient Street

THE STORY OF THE GREAT WALL

Chángchéng de Gùshi

长城的故事

By H. R. Lan (USA)
Photographs by Zhao Bingzhong, Tian Li and Mao Yaoquan

The Great Wall of China has for centuries spawned stories, legends and myths. Many people, Chinese and non-Chinese alike, imagine that the Great Wall has always been one single long brick wall that extends from west to east—a gigantic dragon winding up and down the hills on the outskirts of Beijing. However this notion is quite misleading.

When was the Great Wall built and for what purposes? How did it once look? How long is it? What cultural symbol does it represent? And what is the much cherished spirit of the Great Wall?

SECTIONS:

1. Walls of Earlier Dynasties

2. The Ming Great Wall

3. Why It Was Built

4. Cultural Symbol and World Heritage

5. Legends of the Great Wall

1 Walls of Earlier Dynasties

Zǎoqī Chángchéng

早期长城

Like ancient Rome, the Great Wall of China was not built in a day. Commonly known as *Wan Li Changcheng* in Chinese (万里长城), it was in fact built over twenty centuries of Chinese history, spanning the Spring and Autumn Period (722 BC-481 BC) and the Warring States Period (475 BC-221 BC) to the Ming Dynasty (1368-1644).

Chu Great Wall

As archeological records reveal, primitive Chinese settlers built stretches of walls to protect their settlements as early as the twenty-first century BC. When Chinese society entered the Spring and Autumn and the Warring States periods, the Great Wall gradually took shape. In the beginning scholars believe walls were built primarily to mark territories. But as fierce wars raged continuously, the "Seven Powers" of Qi (齐), Chu (楚), Yan (燕), Han (韩), Zhao (赵), Wei (魏), and Qin (秦) each built walls as military fortifications, connecting beacon towers, pass towers, fortresses, ditches, even exploiting valleys and cliffs. Along with the escalation of war, these defensive walls were extended to stretch out in all directions, crossing many regions and areas in northern China like a huge spider web.

The first part of the Great Wall of China was arguably built by the Chu State. The Chu State was small, gradually developing by defeating weaker neighbors during the Spring and Autumn Period. To prevent the intrusion of the Jin and Qi states, the Chu State built walls as boundary markers along its northern frontier around 656 BC, which were to eventually evolve into the Great Wall. In the shape of the letter "U," the wall of the Chu State was conventionally referred to as "the Rectangle Wall of Chu." (楚方城)

Following the Chu State, the other warring states built their own walls. With the exception of the Wall of Chu in the Yangtze River valley, all the others were in the Yellow River valley or Northern China. Let us look at some

Han Great Wall

of the major ones.

First, the construction of the Wall of the Qi State lasted about 300 years, started in the middle of the Spring and Autumn Period, and was completed in during the Warring States Period. Stretching across almost the whole of today's Shandong Province, the wall was about 650 kilometers long and was later known as the Famous Wall of Qi. With its formidable beacon towers,

Qin Great Wall

Rome wasn't built in a day, and neither was the Great Wall.

ramparts and fortresses, it formed one of the most sophisticated military defenses in ancient China.

The Wall of the Yan State had two sections: the Southern Wall of Yan (燕南长城), also known as the Wall of the River Yi (易水长城), and the Northern Wall of Yan (燕北长城). The former was constructed from 334 BC to 311 BC to prevent attacks from the states of Zhao, Qi and Qin, whereas the latter was built in 254 BC to guard against invasions by nomadic tribes such as the Donghu (东胡). The Wall of Northern Yan, the last wall built in the Warring States Period went all the way through present-day Zhangjiakou City of Hebei Province, Inner Mongolia, across Hebei Province, Chaoyang City of Liaoning Province, over Mt. Yiwulu, and reaching Liaoyang of Liaoning Province. Ruins of the Wall of Yan can still be found in these areas today.

Similarly, the Wall of the Zhao State was also built in two sections. One section, the Southern Wall of Zhao, was built to the south of Zhao in 333 BC to prevent invasion from the states of Wei and later the Qin. Its site can now be seen in Linzhang County and Cixian County of Hebei Province. Located in what is now Inner Mongolia, the other section was built in 300 BC by Duke Zhao Wuling to guard against attacks from the *Hu* nomads. According to historical records, Duke Zhao was a wise ruler who tried to learn from his enemies while fighting against them. Amongst other things, he wore *Hu* garments and learned archery and how to ride horses. As a result, he promoted cultural exchange between nations.

When Qin Shi Huang (秦始皇 259 BC - 210 BC) finally subjugated all the other six Warring States and became the first emperor of a united China, many old walls and fortifications were dismantled. To replace them, Emperor Qin Shi Huang reinforced and renovated the walls built by the former states of Qin, Zhao and Yan, and at the same time added several new sections to form what is now the present-day Great Wall. The newly expanded Wall under the Qin Dynasty more than doubled the original length of the old walls, taking nine years to finish and reaching over ten thousand *li*. Hence, the Great Wall is often referred as *Wang Li Changcheng* in Chinese and throughout history it has been generally associated with or simply attributed to Qin Shi Huang.

However, in terms of length, the longest of the Walls was the one built during the Western Han Dynasty (206 BC- 220 AD). Augmenting the Qin Dynasty Wall, two major parts were added to the Han Dynasty Wall: the Wall of Hexi (河西长城), extending from today's Lanzhou in Gansu Province to Ku'erle in Xinjiang Uygur Autonomous Region, and the Wall of Monan (漠南长城), extending from Huade County in Inner Mongolia to Jinta County in Gansu Province. In fact, the much expanded Han Dynasty Wall was the largest and longest in Chinese history, running from east to west across today's northern Korea and the Chinese provinces and regions of Liaoning, Inner Mongolia, Hebei, Ningxia, Gansu, and Xinjiang, reaching a total length of over 10,000 kilometers.

CHINESE YOU NEED

万里长城 Wànlǐ Chángchéng
Ten-thousand-*li* Long Wall

春秋战国时代 Chūnqiū Zhànguó shídài
The Spring and Autumn and the Warring States periods

秦始皇 Qín Shǐhuáng
Qin Shi Huang

Jiayu Pass

2 The Ming Great Wall

Míng Chángchéng

明长城

A century of change
Adam Warwick and William Lindesay took photos of the Juyong Great Wall in 1922 (left) and 2005 (right page), respectively.

The modern Great Wall was shaped during the Ming Dynasty (1368-1644), during which the Wall was repaired and rebuilt by almost all Ming emperors over a period of 270 years. During this period, bricks, stone and granite blocks were used in sophisticated designs and strong passes were built in places of strategic importance. To strengthen the military control of the northern frontiers, Ming authorities divided the Great Wall into nine zones and placed each under the control of a garrison headquarters. Although reduced in total length (7300 kilometers), the Ming Wall, was the grandest in scale and the most advanced in engineering. It starts from the Yalu River in northeast China and ends at Qilian Mountain in Gansu Province, passing through nine provinces and areas—Liaoning, Hebei, Tianjin, Beijing, Shanxi, Inner

Mongolia, Shaanxi, Ningxia and Gansu. In order to guard against the repeated invasions from Mongolian forces that had been driven out of Central China, the Ming rulers spared no efforts in devoting funding and human resources to fortify the Wall.

Over the span of nearly three centuries, new beacon towers, watch towers, fortresses, tunnels and ditches were constructed along the old walls of Northern Wei, Northern Qi and Sui dynasties using the latest civil engineering methods and building materials. Unlike the walls of earlier dynasties, the Ming Wall had many important passes, including the famous Shanhai Pass (山海关) at the east end, Juyong Pass (居庸关) near Beijing, Yanmen Pass (雁门关) near today's Shanxi Province and Jiayu Pass (嘉峪关) at the west end which, together with the newly designed watch

HOW LONG IS THE GREAT WALL?

How long exactly is the Great Wall? What condition is it in? How are the conditions of the Walls built in different times? These questions are expected to be answered more accurately in the next few years.

It was reported that a survey of the resources of the Great Wall co-sponsored by China State Administration of Cultural Heritage and the State Bureau of Surveying and Mapping has been under-taking since April 2007 covering 13 provinces. The survey would take 4 years to complete. In the first two years the main focus would be on surveying the Great Wall built during the Ming Dynasty (1368-1644); in the following two years a survey of the Walls built in other periods will be conducted and initial work will be completed on compiling the archives and database of the Great Wall.

The Great Wall is the largest cultural heritage site in the world and one of the most magnificent buildings in history. In 1987, the Great Wall as a whole was enlisted by UNESCO as a World Heritage.

towers (空心塔楼), made the Wall even more majestic and effective. Significantly, during the three centuries of the Ming Dynasty, the construction of the Great Wall was never neglected or weakened and its importance and grandeur exceeded that of earlier periods.

As shown by the ruins scattered in northern China, the walls of past dynasties and states were built in various shapes and designs, using materials available near the construction sites. Near Beijing the walls were constructed from quarried limestone blocks; in other locations, quarried granite or fired bricks. Still others used masonry, stones and packed-earth. In some areas the blocks were cemented with a mixture of glutinous rice and egg white. In the extreme western desert locations, where good materials were scarce, the walls were built from earth rammed between rough wood tied together with woven reed mats. Like the ancient Egyptians building the Great Pyramid, ancient Chinese laborers invented many new construction techniques during the long and arduous process. According to legend, they invented the first method of making cement; they used goats to carry the heavy bricks to the top; they paved roads of ice to move millions of heavy stone blocks in bitter winter; they discovered numerous ways to save time, expense and labor, a grand tribute to human ingenuity.

Interestingly, throughout the long history of China only three dynasties were not involved in rebuilding the Wall. They were the Tang (618-907), Yuan (1206-1368), and the Qing dynasties (1616-1911). The reasons are easy to understand: China under Tang rule was the most powerful nation militarily and economically in the world, and its rulers were not worried about foreign invasions. In fact, neighboring kingdoms and tribes, in awe of Tang military and economic strength, regularly paid tribute to the Tang court. As for the Yuan and Qing dynasties, they were non-Han peoples, Mongol and Manchu respectively, and didn't have the traditional commitment to the Great Wall.

CHINESE YOU NEED

八达岭长城 Bādálǐng Cháng chéng
Badaling Great Wall

The Great Wall as we know it today was constructed mostly during the Ming Dynasty.

3 Why It Was Built

Zuòyòng hé Mùdì
作用和目的

Why are such colossal walls unique to China? What role did the Wall really play in history? And how do we look at the Wall today? To answer these questions, we need to briefly revisit the history and geography of China.

First, with a total area of 9.6 million sq km, China is a vast land that shares an exceptionally long border with its neighbors. This unique geographic feature alone made it both possible and important to build a gigantic project like the Great Wall. Second, unlike the Great Pyramid in ancient Egypt, whose true function remains a mystery, from the beginning the Great Wall was built with a clear purpose—as a military defense system.

Historically speaking, the neighbors of the so-called Central Plains (中原) in the North and Northeast were nomads whose way of life differed drastically from that of the Central Plains. Therefore, almost from the beginning, the Great Wall served as a demarcation line between two cultures and two modes of production—an agricultural society on the south and a nomad society on the north side of the Wall. In the South, the climate was mild, rainy and warm—suitable for agriculture; people grew crops, lived in houses, clustered in villages; whereas in the North, the climate was cold, harsh and dry, unsuitable for agriculture; people herded cattle, sheep and horses, lived in tents, caravans and on horseback and frequently moved about to search for pasture land.

Thus it is not hard to imagine why the nomads in the North wanted to expand and attack the South. As history witnessed, those neighboring nomad tribes were a constant military threat to the southern agricultural society; during those years when the climate was unusually severe, fierce military conflicts occurred between the Chinese settlers in the Central Plains and the

nomad tribes of the North and Northeast. Many such conflicts, such as the invasions of Qidan (契丹), Nüzhen (女真) and Mongols (蒙古) around the 13th century, and the Manchu (满洲) intrusion during the 17th century, all occurred during years with severe weather conditions.

Ever since Qin Shi Huang united the "Middle Kingdom (中国),"the primary purpose of building a wall had been to guard against frequent invasions, especially during the Ming Dynasty after the overthrow of the Yuan Dynasty established by the Mongolian nomadic tribes, compelling the newly enthroned Ming ruler, Zhu Yuanzhang (朱元璋 1328-1398), to take these threats seriously.

After the founding of the Ming Dynasty in 1368, the Mongolian nobles, refusing to accept defeat, launched several attacks hoping to restore their rule. Emperor Zhu Yuanzhang, who had experience with the peasant uprising, understood the importance of protective walls around cities and along the border. He also saw the Great Wall not only as a national defense but as a symbol of power. Therefore, soon after he came to power, Emperor Zhu Yuanzhang issued orders to build new walls around cities and to fortify and expand the old walls, thus commencing the Herculean task of reconstructing the Great Wall that lasted nearly three centuries under the Ming.

The primary driving force behind such a mission throughout the history of the Great Wall was rooted in the Confucian teaching: "Harmony is most valuable in performing rites" (礼之用，和为贵). Fundamentally influenced by Confucianism, a philosophy that stresses interpersonal relationships based on virtues like benevolence (仁), loyalty (义), magnanimity (恕), and righteousness (礼), the Chinese people have always cherished "Peace and Harmony." The Great Wall is the embodiment of such a goal, as a barrier against chaos.

Dynasty after dynasty, generation after generation, China built and rebuilt the Wall at enormous cost in resources and human lives. The Great Wall was built to prevent foreign intrusions, to defend national territory, to protect people's livelihood, to guarantee social stability and economic development; basically to seek peace and harmony among nations and peoples. Throughout Chinese history many of China's rulers expended great effort to achieve peace with their neighbors, frequently adopting the policy of "making peace through marriage." (和亲) There have been many such good-will marriages, the most well-known are those of Lady Wang Zhaojun (王昭君) in the Han Dynasty and Princess Wencheng (文成公主) in the Tang Dynasty. Significantly, these interracial and cross-cultural marriages proved to be successful and played an important role in promoting the social, economic and cultural ties between peoples.

4

Cultural Symbol and World Heritage

Wénhuà Xiàngzhēng hé Shìjiè Yíchǎn

文化象征和世界遗产

Over the past twenty centuries, the Great Wall has weathered storms and witnessed not only wars and conflicts but also peace, integration, development and cultural exchange. Today, swords have turned into ploughshares; as a result, the ethnic groups of China are now able to co-existence peacefully and harmoniously.

Standing magnificently in the northern mountains and valleys of China, the Great Wall is one of the largest construction projects on earth. Its total accumulated length reaches over one hundred thousand kilometers. Even today, the remaining Wall is still over 5,000 kilometers long, its thickness ranging from about 4.5 to 9 meters and its height up to 8 meters. Although it cannot be seen from the moon—contrary to a popular belief—the Great Wall of China is indeed visible from orbiting spacecraft, as witnessed by American astronaut Neil Armstrong and others.

On the merits and demerits of the Great Wall, Dr. Sun Yat-sen (孙中山), Father of the 1911 Chinese Revolution, once said: "In spite of the tyranny of Qin Shi Huang, the Great Wall built under his rule has proved beneficial for generations, its significance equaling that of Great Yu's Flood Control Project (大禹治水). Without the Great Wall as its staunch guard, China would have been conquered by its northern neighbours as early as the time of Qin and Chu (in the Warring States Period), and there would never have been the development and prosperity of the dynasties of the Han and Tang and the consequent unity with ethnic groups in the south (of China)." Undoubtedly, without the Great Wall there would not have been the splendid cultural past of ancient China.

Today, the Great Wall no longer serves as a military fortification; instead, it has become one of the most favoured tourist attractions in China and the world. Since the official opening of the Badaling (八达岭) section in Beijing's outskirts in 1957, more than 300 heads of state have visited the Great Wall. For this section alone, millions of tourists are received annually. Presidents, queens, ministers, workers, farmers, students, and soldiers alike, they all stand on the Wall in awe of this ancient architectural wonder.

As time passes, the Great Wall becomes even more a cultural symbol of the national spirit of China. It symbolizes Chinese people's love for peace and progress; and it crystallizes hope for stability and harmony. But there is much more to it. Officially recognized as a UNESCO World Heritage Site in 1987, the Great Wall has been imbued with a new significance and mission. No longer merely the national pride of China, the Great Wall, recognized as a world legacy, is viewed as a testimony to human ingenuity, perseverance and dignity, carrying a profound sense of mission for eternal world peace, prosperity and solidarity.

5 Legends of the Great Wall

Chángchéng de Chuánshuō

长城的传说

I. THE TEARS OF LADY MENG JIANG, THE FALL OF THE GREAT WALL
孟姜女哭长城(Mèngjiāngnǔ Kū Chángchéng)

A long, long time ago, in the Qin Dynasty, there lived a young girl named Meng Jiang. Hers was a quiet and happy life, together with her parents in a small village in northern China. Meng Jiang was pretty, amiable and always willing to lend a helping hand. All her fellow villagers adored her and often called her Lady Meng Jiang. At the tender age of 17, she was married to a fine young man, Fan Xiliang.

But, unfortunately, their bliss didn't last long. Soon after they were married, the Imperial Army came to their village with orders from Emperor Qin Shi Huang, "One man from each family is to serve the Emperor in his construction of the Great Wall." Thus, Fan Xiliang, was among the many young men of the village, conscripted and forced to leave his wife and home to build the Great Wall.

A smart and sensible young woman, Lady Meng Jiang was well aware of how dangerous building the Great Wall was, and deeply worried about her husband. She prayed to God in Heaven every day and night for her husband's quick return. But years went by without her hearing a single word from or about him.

Determined, Lady Meng Jiang set out on a journey in search for her beloved. Carrying a new coat she had made for him, she trudged for months on the rocky paths and mountains that made up the Great Wall. As she walked, she asked everyone she met if they knew her husband. But to her dismay, no one did, nor did they have any knowledge of his whereabouts. At long last, she stumbled upon the men from her village. But when she asked about her husband, her biggest fear came true: Fan Xiliang had died long ago of starvation and exhaustion. Upon hearing the tragic news, Lady Meng Jiang fainted. When she came to, she went to her husband's burial site and cried. Her tears dropped on the Wall, day and night, until it began to crumble. After three days and nights, the Wall and Lady Meng Jiang collapsed, and she was buried next to her beloved.

The story of *The Tears of Lady Meng Jiang and the Fall of the Great Wall* has endured for centuries. To this day, visitors to the Shanhai Pass in Qinhuangdao (秦皇岛) can visit the exact place where Lady Meng Jiang's sorrow proved to great to bear.

Illustration by Mark Ma

II. BAO SI AND THE BEACON TOWER BONFIRE

褒姒和烽火台(Bāo Sì hé Fēnghuǒtái)

The Great Wall is home to countless spectacular beacon towers. In ancient times, they played a key role in military communication. When enemy troops pressed towards the border, signals from the towers were sent via bonfires during the night and smoke in the day.

An old tale about the beacon towers involves the beauty Queen Bao Si and her cold demeanor..

Although not born into wealth, Bao Si was one of the most beautiful women of the state of Bao. After King You of the Western Zhou Dynasty (1046 BC - 771 BC) conquered Bao, Bao Si was presented to the King. King You fell in love with Bao Si immediately, and in no time made her his concubine. However, Bao Si was perpetually unhappy, and even though he tried everything in his power, King You could never make her smile.

"My dear concubine, what on earth are you fond of?" the King eagerly asked.

"I don't fancy anything, but when I was a child, I liked to listen to the sound of silk being torn. It was so pleasant," she replied.

So, the King ordered several maids of honor to tear rolls of colored silk for her amusement every day. At first Bao Si seemed pleased but her amusement proved fleeting. Soon she tired of her childhood joy.

"Why don't you ever smile, my dear?" the King asked impatiently.

"I don't know." Bao Si replied.

The King tried and tried again but to no avail. Finally, he offered a prize to his people: "Anyone who can amuse Concubine Bao Si will be awarded with 1,000 pieces of gold."

Soon, a cunning court official presented an idea to the King, "Why don't your majesties set a bonfire on the beacon tower and trick those dukes?" Pleased with the advice of his countryman, that night, after he and Bao Si had reached Lishan Mountain by carriage, King You gave the order. Soon the flames of the bonfire were lighting up the sky above the beacon tower. Seeing the fire signal, all the dukes thought there was an emergency, and moved their troops immediately to Lishan Mountain to assist the King. But to their great surprise, when they arrived, they found the King and Bao Si drinking, without a care in the world. When asked for an explanation, the King offered, "Nothing has happened. I simply played a joke on you to please my concubine." Upon hearing this, Bao Si burst into laughter, looking as pretty and charming as ever. The cunning official was rewarded with 1,000 pieces of gold. Later, King You was to repeat the joke several times, and each time, needless to say, the dukes felt cheated and very angry.

In 771 BC, when a northern nomad tribe staged a real attack against Western Zhou, King You urgently ordered the beacon tower set on fire, but this time none of the dukes came to his rescue. As a result, King You was killed, Bao Si captured, and the Western Zhou Dynasty was no more.

Hence the saying: "Even with a thousand pieces of gold, a smile doesn't come cheap." (千金难买一笑).

III. LADY WANG ZHAOJUN GOES NORTH OF THE GREAT WALL

昭君出塞(Zhāojūn Chū Sài)

Everyone in China knows the four great beauties of ancient China: Xi Shi (西施) of the Warring States Period, Diao Chan (貂蝉) of the Three Kingdoms Period, Wang Zhaojun (王昭君) of the Western Han, and Lady Yang (杨贵妃) of the Tang Dynasty.

Of the four great beauties, Lady Wang Zhaojun was considered "a political bride," whose name today stands not only for physical beauty but also for goodwill in bridging nations and cultures.

During the reign of the Emperor Xuan (73BC-49 BC), the Xiongnu (匈奴), the Han's troublesome northern neighbor, split into five kingdoms, each led by a chieftain known as a Chanyu (单于). In a bid for control, the five Chanyus fought amongst themselves. When Chanyu Khukhenye, was defeated by his brother Chanyu Zhizhi-Guduhu, he decided to make peace with a former foe to the south, Emperor Xuan, and paid him a personal visit.

Pleased by his offer to meet, Emperor Xuan went out of his way to meet Khukhenye in his capital, Chang'an, and held a grand banquet in his former foe's honor. After a month's stay in Chang'an, Khukhenye longed to return home and asked Emperor Xuan for help. The emperor sent an army of 10,000 men to escort him and gave him 100,000 bushels of food for his people. The thankful Khukhenye determined it would be wise to maintain a friendly relationship with the Han Dynasty.

Emperor Xuan was succeeded by his son, Emperor Yuan. In the year of 33BC, Chanyu Khukhenye returned to the Han capital. After arriving he asked to marry one of Emperor Yuan's daughters in order to cement the relations between the Han and Xiongnu people. The emperor agreed to allow him to marry a maid of honor. However, only one maid of honor was willing to enter a marriage that would require her to leave Han. That maid was Wang Zhaojun, an exceptionally beautiful and intelligent young lady.

At the wedding ceremony Emperor Yuan, upon noticing how beautiful Wang Zhaojun was, began to regret his decision. After much inner-debate, Emperor Yuan blessed the marriage out of a sense of duty and admiration for Zhaojun's courage and selflessness.

Wang Zhaojun then embarked on the long journey to Xiongnu. She and her escorts braved bitter cold and heavy sandstorms and snowstorms before finally reaching their destination. There she was given the title "Lady Yanzhi: the Peacemaker" (宁胡阏氏) in the hope that she would bring her adopted land peace and security. Thanks to Wang Zhaojun's goodwill, encouragement and vision, Khukhenye abandoned its violent ways, and peace prospered on the border between the Han and the Xiongnu for over half a century.

Illustration by Mark Ma

SHAOLIN MONASTERY TODAY

Jīnrì Shàolín
今日少林

By Liu Xin
Photographs by Mao Yaoquan
Translated by Wei Lingcha

Shaolin Monastery is more than 1,500 years old. What is it like today? What kind of life do the monks live? Is Shaolin Kung Fu really as magical as movies and books portray it? Well, let's have a look.

Practicing kung fu in front of the Stupa Forest

SECTIONS:

1. Approaching Shaolin Monastery **2.** The Source of Kung Fu

Main gate of the Shaolin Monastery

SECTIONS:

3. Shaolin Culture Goes Global

4. A Monk's Life

1 Approaching Shaolin Monastery

Zǒujìn Shàolín Sì
走进少林寺

All fans of Chinese kung fu have heard of Shaolin Monastery. Where is it? What are the stories and legends about it? Here are some answers.

In central China, nestled in the wooded mountains of Dengfeng, Henan stands an ancient Buddhist monastery, which was first built in AD 495 during the Northern Wei Dynasty (北魏，386-534). Legend has it that Northern Wei Emperor Xiaowen (北魏孝文帝), a believer in Buddhism, had a monastery built for the Indian dhyana monk Buddhabhadra (跋陀) on the side of Mount Shaoshi (少室山) of the Song Mountains (嵩山). The monastery, often referred to as Shaolin Temple, got its name "Shaolin" (少林) because it was nestled in the thick woods (林) of Mount Shaoshi. The second celebrated monk of the monastery was Bodhidharma (菩提达摩，?-528/536), also from India. He was the founder of Chan Buddhism (Zen), a very important sect of Chinese Buddhism. After Bodhidharma, the monastery experienced a growth in the number of monks and in reputation and influence. It is reputed to be the cradle of Chan Buddhism.

Shaolin Monastery stands at the foot of the mountain. Inside the main gate is a seven-compound complex where the monks worship the Buddha (拜佛), sit in meditation (坐禅), chant sutras (诵经), receive guests, store books, hold services and live.

Qianfo (literally "Thousand Buddha") Hall (千佛殿), built in 1588, is the largest structure in the monastery. Entering it, you will be overwhelmed by the ancient fresco entitled *Five Hundred Arhats Worshiping Vairocana Buddha* (《五百罗汉朝毗卢》). Each arhat in the painting has its own expression and distinctive characteristics, thus lending abundant interest to the work. In addition to Qianfo Hall, the Baiyi (literally "White Clothes") Hall (白衣殿) also contains some frescos which depict monks practicing martial arts (武术).

Part frescos in the Qianfo Hall

Stele marking the Mingling of three relegions

In the monastery stand many steles that record its culture, history and glory. A typical stele here is called *Ode to the Mingling of Different Schools* (《混元三教九流图赞》). Carved on the stele is an old man, whose façade appears to be Sakyamuni (释迦牟尼), founder of Buddhism; to his left, Confucius (孔子), founder of Confucianism, and right, Lao Tze (老子), founder of Taoism. The trinity of the three figures illuminates the essence of Chinese culture: profound and tolerant, drawing on the strengths and quintessence of varying schools.

About 300 meters to the west of the monastery is the Stupa Forest (塔林) which enshrines the remains of more than 250 abbots. Of different sizes and shapes, the stupas all bear inscriptions and carvings. This area has served as the cemetery for the abbots since the Tang Dynasty (唐朝, 618-907). Being the largest of its kind in China, the Stupa Forest provides rare information for research in ancient Chinese brick-and-stone structures and carvings.

Equally important in the history of classical temple and monastery architecture are Xilai (literally "Arriving from the West") Hall (西来堂), the Hall of Heavenly Kings (天王殿), the Mahavira Hall (大雄宝殿), the Bell Tower (钟楼), and the Drum Tower (鼓楼).

CHINESE YOU NEED

寺 sì
monastery

碑 bēi
stele

塔 tǎ
pagoda

FOLKLORE

THIRTEEN STAFF-WIELDING MONKS RESCUING THE TANG EMPEROR

The closing years of the Sui Dynasty (隋朝，581-618) witnessed great political instability. Li Shimin (李世民), then King Qin, launched an expedition against Wang Shichong (王世充), a separatist warlord. The martial monks at the Shaolin Monastery were invited to assist Li. It so happened that Li became the second emperor of the Tang Dynasty, i.e. Emperor Taizong (唐太宗). This event is later referred to as "13 Monks Rescuing the Tang Emperor (十三棍僧救唐王)." The film *Shaolin Temple* (《少林寺》), which was based on this story, caught the imagination of the Chinese, at home and abroad. When Li Shimin was enthroned, he generously rewarded the monks and allowed the monastery the privilege of keeping and training a group of monk soldiers. Thanks to the royal patronage, the Shaolin Monastery developed into a world-famous Buddhist monastery. It reached its zenith during the Ming Dynasty (明朝，1368-1644).

Dharma Cave

BODHIDHARMA AND SHAOLIN MONASTERY

Legend has it that Bodhidharma arrived in Guangzhou in AD 527 after a three-year trip from India. When Emperor Wu (梁武帝) of the Liang Dynasty (南朝梁，502-557) learned of this, he sent an envoy to bring Bodhidharma to Nanjing. Unfortunately, the two didn't agree with each other; so, Bodhidharma crossed the Yangtze River borne up by a reed leaf. Finally he reached the Shaolin Monastery, where he spent nine years sitting in meditation in a cave he had carved out in the Wuru (literally "Five-Breast") Peak (五乳峰). The cave, now called Dharma Cave (达摩洞), has been a tourist attraction to this day.

Outside the Chuzu (literally "First Patriarch") Hall (初祖殿), there is also a pavilion named after Bodhidharma, also known as Lixue (literally "Standing in the Snow") Pavilion (立雪亭). It is said that in AD 520, a monk named Shenguang (神光) came to the pavilion for instruction only to be ignored by Bodhidharma who was meditating. Although it was a cold and snowy winter day, Shenguang waited patiently outside in knee-deep snow for a whole night. Bodhidharma turned a blind eye to all this, saying "I won't take you as my disciple unless it snows red snow." To express his sincerity, Shenguang cut off his left arm with a sharp knife. Immediately his blood dyed the snow on the ground red and the falling snowflakes also seemed red because of the reflection. Touched by his determination, Bodhidharma conferred upon him his robe and bowl (衣钵) and gave him the Buddhist name (法名) Huike (慧可, literally 'Enlightenable'). Huike later became the second patriarch of the Shaolin Monastery. And the place where he healed his wound was given the name Arm-Healing Stand (养臂台).

禪

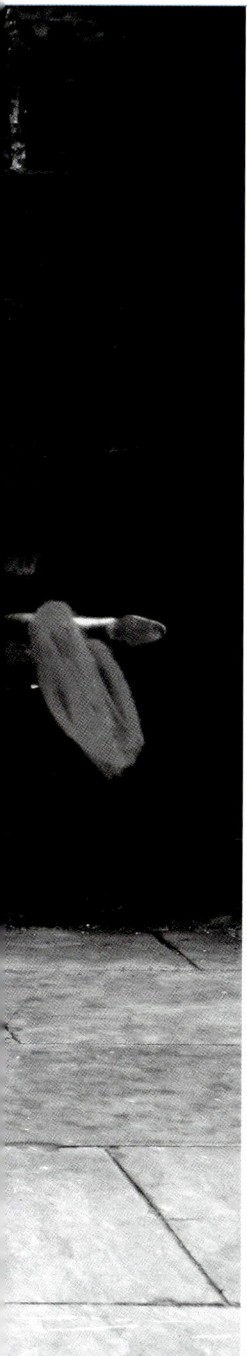

2 The Source of Kung Fu

"Tiānxià Gōngfu Chū Shàolín"

"天下功夫出少林"

It is universally acknowledged that the Shaolin Monastery is the source of all kung fu around the world. What is the reason for this belief? Why did the monks here practice kung fu? What is the essence of kung fu?

Fresco in the Baiyi Hall

There is a legend about the origin of Shaolin Kung Fu. When Patriarch Bodhidharma sat crossed-legged in meditation for long hours, he would suffer physical pains and discomfort. To relax, he created a regime of exercise. After that, the Shaolin monks developed a habit of physical training via martial arts.

Shaolin Kung Fu takes martial arts techniques and routine moves as its form of expression and Buddhist beliefs and Chan enlightenment as its content. Shaolin Kung Fu is first and foremost a belief, a pursuit of superhuman power. This is the very reason why Shaolin Kung Fu is considered so miraculous. This is also what distinguishes it from other styles of martial arts.

In Shaolin Kung Fu, the combination of Chan Buddhism and martial arts (禅武合一) is highly valued. The Chan sect of Buddhism was the result of the mingling of Buddhism with Chinese metaphysics (玄学). Hence Chan is the crystallization of two ancient oriental cultures. The emergence of Chan made the otherwise complex Buddhist doctrines direct and simple and the otherwise mysterious monastic regimen easily applicable. Chan draws on the thoughts of distinguished monks and philosophers through the ages about either the secrets of the universe or the truth of life. Shaolin Kung Fu practitioners are mainly Chan Buddhists, who are disciplined by Buddhist doctrines as well by martial ethics. Hence Shaolin Kung Fu has always been characterized by temperance, internal energy, and passive defensive moves. In dealing with an opponent, Shaolin monks follow the Eight Attacks and Eight Restraints (八打八不打), i.e., attacking the eight parts of the body which are vulnerable but not vital while sparing the eight vital parts. This is a distinctive feature of Shaolin Kung Fu. Of course, martial ethics is by no means exclusive to Shaolin Kung Fu. It is stressed by all other schools of Chinese kung fu. Among

Shaolin Kung Fu practitioners are mainly Chan Buddhists, disciplined by Buddhist doctrines and martial ethics.

An ordination ceremony in the Chan Hall

their values are "cultivating both mind and body" (身心双修), "making friends through martial arts" (以武会友), "stopping short of causing injury" (点到即止), refraining from deadly blows.

Shaolin Kung Fu has an enormous array of techniques. The illustrated boxing manuals that have survived to this day record 708 sets of routine moves, which are combined into a large and orderly system in terms of categories and degrees of difficulty. The transition from one move to another in the routine not only follows the laws of human physical kinetics but also abundantly embodies the philosophical ideas in Chinese culture such as the balance of yin and yang (阴阳平衡), harmony of toughness and flexibility (刚柔相济), and integration of man and nature (天人合一).

The patriarchal system, which was based on blood relations, is an important feature of traditional Chinese culture. The Confucian concepts of the unity of the state and the family and the unity of loyalty to the monarch and filial piety find their way into every corner of society, including the Shaolin Monastery. Shaolin Kung Fu is passed down strictly from master to pupil. In the course of learning it, although the pupil can follow the instructional chart of the movements in his training, high level Shaolin Kung Fu can only be attained through the master's individual coaching and the pupil's enlightenment from meditation and monastic regimen.

CHINESE YOU NEED

禅 chán
Chan buddhism

武 wǔ
martial art

功夫 gōngfu
kung fu

Stone carvings of *Yi Jin Jing*

禪武合一

In Shaolin Kung Fu, the combination of Chan Buddhism and martial arts is highly valued. The Chan sect of Buddhism was the result of the mingling of Buddhism with Chinese metaphysics.

Kung fu field

3

Shaolin Culture Goes Global

Shàolín Wénhuà Tiānxià Chuán

少林文化天下传

In a myriad of ways, Shaolin culture reveals to the secular world the inner spiritual world of the new generation of monks here, endearing itself to more and more people.

少林寺

1982 witnessed the release of the martial arts feature film *Shaolin Temple* (《少林寺》) starring Jet Li, which made the then long-forgotten monastery famous far and wide again. In the same year the film was released, the number of tourists visiting the monastery tripled. With the growth of tourism, the monastery has become one of the most famous tourist attractions in China. In recent years the Shaolin Monastery has become increasingly aware of the importance of cultural dissemination. In August 2004, the Monastery made public its secret martial arts manuals on its web site, including *Yi Jin Jing* (《易筋经》, literally "The Muscle Tendon Change Classic"), *Xi Sui Jing* (《洗髓经》, literally "The Marrow Cleansing Classic"), 72 unique skills, acupoint hitting techniques, etc. With it, the Shaolin Monastery again became the focus of the world's martial arts enthusiasts.

Over the past 1,500 years, Shaolin Monastery has developed a cultural system embracing Chan Buddhism, martial arts, medicine, etc. It is now striving to dig deeper into and disseminate Shaolin Kung Fu culture. To this end, the monastery has set up its Martial Monk Team (武僧团), Shaolin Martial Arts Library, and the Research Institute of Shaolin Culture and launched the magazine *Chan Lu* (《禅露》, literally "the Dew of Zen") in an attempt to carry out systematic research on Chan, martial arts, medicine, and arts of Shaolin culture. Additionally, to market Shaolin Kung Fu in China and around the world, the monastery held an international symposium on Shaolin Kung Fu, staged plays about Shaolin Kung Fu and produced animated Shaolin Kung Fu cartoons with other cultural and artistic groups.

When the Martial Monk Team was restored, its function shifted to promoting kung fu culture by performing Shaolin Kung Fu. Since 1988 when the team made its début, it has traveled to more than 40 countries and regions around the world. Gradually kung fu performances have become an indispensable component of China's international cultural exchange programs.

Lixue Pavilion

A bronze statue displaying *jingluo* (meridian and collateral channels) in front of Shaolin Pharmacy

A child trains at the martial arts school near the Shaolin Monastery

In recent years, the Shaolin Monastery has placed great importance on preserving Shaolin medicinal practices. Upon arrival at the main gate of the monastery, the tourists see a classical courtyard house with the signboard 少林药局 (Shaolin Pharmacy). Shaolin medicine has a history of over 1,000 years and has developed into a distinctive school referred to reverently as the "Shaolin Model of Medicine" and the Shaolin Pharmacy is called the "Medicinal Sect of Chinese Buddhism." Recently the monastery has been further cataloging and developing the secret Shaolin prescriptions and remedies.

In 2006, the Shaolin Monastery produced a big-budget musical called *Chan Buddhism at Shaolin: A Grand Ritual of Music* (《禅宗少林•音乐大典》), and staged it in the Daixian (literally "Waiting for the Immortal") Valley (待仙沟) of the Shaoshi peak, seven kilometers from the monastery. The Shaolin monks sang in an entirely natural surrounding, with Chan music accompanied by various sounds of nature in the valley: water flowing, wind whistling, trees rustling, and insects chirping. They combined as the very Chan rhythm of nature. Assisted by the marvelous combination of music, dance, lights, and kung fu, the audience enjoyed a feast of unique Shaolin culture.

In a myriad of ways, the deep-rooted Shaolin culture reveals to the secular world the inner spiritual world of the new generation of monks here, endearing both Shaolin Kung Fu and Chinese culture to an increasing number of people.

CHINESE YOU NEED

电影 diànyǐng
movie

演出 yǎnchū
performance

药局 yàojú
pharmacy

Performance of A Grand Ritual of Music

STARS IN KUNG FU MOVIES
功夫电影明星

Bruce Lee
李小龙 Lǐ Xiǎolóng

A martial artist, kung fu movie star, and the founder of Jeet Kune Do (截拳道), Bruce Lee's "down-to-earth" performances in movies captured the imagination of international audiences and thus linger on in the memory of lovers of Chinese kung fu. Among his masterpieces are *Fists of Fury* (《唐山大兄》) and *The Chinese Connection* (《精武门》).

Jet Li
李连杰 Lǐ Liánjié

Jet Li won the all-round gold medal at the Fifth National Wushu (Chinese word for "martial arts") Championship at the early age of 11. He came to international prominence when he starred in *Shaolin Temple* in 1982. His leading role in *Wong Fei Hung* (《黄飞鸿》) established his reputation as a martial arts movie star. His recent movies include *Hero* (《英雄》), *Fearless* (《霍元甲》), etc.

Jackie Chan
成龙 Chéng Lóng

The roles Jackie Chan plays are typically those of "little potatoes." So he appears more approachable than those great kung fu masters in previous kung fu movies. His movies are characterized by thrills and humor. His masterpieces include *Police Story* (《警察故事》), *Rumble in the Bronx* and *Rush Hour*.

Michelle Yeoh
杨紫琼
Yáng Zǐqióng

Yeoh is the most influential female kung fu movie star in Hong Kong. Among her masterpieces are *007: Tomorrow Never Dies* and *Crouching Tiger, Hidden Dragon* (《卧虎藏龙》). Her role in *007: Golden Eye* depicted her as "the first Bond girl who could fight James Bond."

The Shaolin monks tour Washington D. C.

4 A Monk's Life

Shàolín Sēngrén de Shēnghuó

少林僧人的生活

The monks here attend morning classes in the Mahavira Hall at 4 every morning. Then they have breakfast.

To the dinning hall

Calligraphy is good for Chan meditation

There are civil monks and martial monks in the Shaolin Monastery. The martial monks are versed in Buddhism, skilled in kung fu and enthusiastic about Shaolin culture. Like other monks, their daily schedule includes morning class, evening class, meditation, and Buddhist study. In addition, they undergo about four hours of kung fu training.

The morning class begins in the Mahavira Hall at 4 am. After breakfast, the monks sit in meditation, practice martial arts, attend to monastic affairs and receive tourists. Novice monks have cultural classes in the morning on a daily basis. Courses include scripture study, Chinese, math, history, geography, and English. The monks started learning English long ago. In the side halls, novice monks can be seen reading English out loud. At 5 pm, all the monks gather in Mahavira Hall again for evening class.

The Shaolin Monastery values cultural exchange. Over the past few years, the Monastery has established branch monasteries or culture centers in many countries and regions. In the last 20 years, nearly ten thousand lovers of Shaolin Kung Fu from over 80 countries have made pilgrimages to this holy monastery in Mount Song. To people of the world who are interested in Chinese culture, Shaolin culture is a symbol of Buddhist culture in China and a symbol of traditional Chinese culture. In a sense, Shaolin culture serves as a bridge linking peoples around the world.

CHINESE YOU NEED

僧人 sēngrén
monk

交流 jiāoliú
cultural exchange

Quanzhou Shaolin Monastery

OTHER SHAOLIN MONASTERIES
少林寺外的少林

It is generally known that the first Shaolin Monastery was built in Mount Song in Henan Province. But there is some dispute about how many other Shaolin monasteries there are. One belief is that the Shaolin order falls geographically into two schools: the Northern and the Southern, the former referring to the Shaolin Monastery in Henan, the latter to the three Shaolin monasteries in Putian, Quanzhou and Fuqing in the southern province of Fujian.

In 2002, the Shaolin Monastery confirmed that extensive research had proven that a monastery in Jixian County of Tianjin was the only branch monastery in recorded history. Since it is located to the north of the Shaolin Monastery in Mount Song, it is called the "Northern Shaolin." In addition, the "sub-monastery" of Shaolin, the Kongxiang Monastery (空相寺) situated in the Xiong'er (literally "Bear Ears") Mountain (熊耳山), has also received official recognition from the Shaolin Monastery in the Song Mountains.

MYSTERY OF THE MOUNTAIN MANSION

Shāngōu Lǐ de Huángchéng Xiàngfǔ

山沟里的皇城相府

By Chu Dandan
Photographs by Mao Yaoquan, Li Fuyu
Translated by Wei Lingcha

This interesting treasure is set in a little village called Huangcheng—literally "Royal Residence" —in a remote valley.

In this valley amid the Taihang Mountains in southeastern Shanxi Province is nestled a little village of nearly 700 people. Small as it is, the village has a magnificent name Huangcheng (皇城, "Royal Residence"). Several hundred miles from the real royal residence of Beijing and hardly accessible to the outside world, how has it maintained such a grand and unique name over the centuries?

This mystery was not unraveled until we crossed successive ridges and passed through tunnel after tunnel. When we reached the foot of a high yellowish wall, suddenly we saw a solemn mansion of grand construction snuggled in the embrace of the mountain. This is the Royal Residence of the Premier, a mysterious castle of the Orient.

SECTIONS:

1. What Is the Royal Residence of the Premier?
2. Castle or House?
3. The Birthplace of *The Kangxi Dictionary*
4. Historic Huangcheng Village

1 What Is the Royal Residence of the Premier?

Shénme Jiào "Huángchéng Xiàngfǔ"
什么叫"皇城相府"

The name originated with an emperor and a premier.

Imposing Heshan Tower

The Royal Residence in snow

"皇" (huáng) means "emperor;" the place where an emperor lives is called the Royal Residence. A case in point is the Forbidden City in Beijing. This is a mansion where an emperor once stayed so it's called "a Royal Residence."

The complex used to be the residence of premier Chen Tingjing during the reign of Emperor Kangxi (1662-1722). "相" (xiàng) means "assist" in ancient Chinese. "丞相"(chéngxiàng) is the chief official who assists the emperor to govern the country, or, the prime minister. The titles for such a position vary with different dynasties; however, they have been consistently called "丞相" by the ordinary people. Although the official title for Chen Tingjing was Grand Secretary of Wenyuan Academy and Minister of the Official Personnel Ministry, he actually served as the premier. Thus, his home is called the Premier's Residence.

What's unique about this premier's residence is that Emperor Kangxi stayed here twice. It was very unusual at that time for an emperor to have a tour of inspection outside the capital. But this rare event did happen: Emperor Kangxi, a diligent monarch, not only made an inspection tour but also traveled all the way to the Taihang Mountains and sojourned at the residence of his favorite official. This very place produced a premier and accommodated an emperor, thereby justifying the name Royal Residence of the Premier.

The Genealogy of the Chen Family

CHINESE YOU NEED

皇 huáng
the emperor

相 xiàng
the premier

府 fǔ
the residence

The Palace Graduates of the Chen Family

(Top row left to right):
Chen Tianyou, Chen Changyan, Chen Tingjing, Chen Yuan, Chen Yupeng

(Bottom row left to right):
Chen Zhuanglu,
Chen Guanyong,
Chen Suizhen, Chen Shijian

Inside the Residence of Emperor Kangxi

府 fǔ

THE RESIDENCE

"府" is not a character applied to the house of an ordinary family. In ancient China, it means exclusively the abode of an official or aristocrat. There are, for example, "王府" (lord's residence) and "将军府" (general's residence). Today, the character is applied solely to the office or home of the head of state. Examples: "总统府" (president's home and/or office) and "首相府" (prime minister's home and/or office).

康熙 Kāngxī

EMPEROR KANGXI

The Qing Dynasty (1616-1911), the last feudal monarchy in China, was founded by the Manchu. Kangxi was enthroned as the fourth emperor of the Qing Dynasty at the age of eight (1662). An outstanding statesman, he ruled for 61 years, the longest reign in Chinese history. He ranks as one of the most remarkable monarches in world history like King Louis XIV (1638-1715) of the Bourbon Monarchy in France and Peter the Great (1672-1725) of the Romanov Monarchy in Russia.

During the Kangxi Reign, a powerful China enjoyed prosperity and peace. Kangxi consolidated his control over the frontiers, greatly contributing to national unification and internal unity. Together with Emperor Qianlong, he brought about Kang Qian Sheng Shi: the Great Prosperity of the Kangxi and Qianlong Reigns (1662-1759).

Manchu though he was, Kangxi loved Chinese culture. His extensive interests led him into profound studies of literature, arts and natural science. He ventured to vaccinate his own children against smallpox and advocated the use of quinine against malaria in the court. Importance was also attached to education and culture. He ordered the compilation of a number of voluminous dictionaries, including *The Kangxi Dictionary*.

Although Kangxi was an excellent monarch, his was not a peaceful family life. He fathered 35 sons and 20 daughters but only 24 of his sons and 7 of his daughters survived to adulthood. Even worse was the relentless struggle for power among his sons, intensifying the emperor's fatigue, both mental and physical.

A Watchtower in rain

2 Castle or House?

Shì Jiāzhái Háishi Chéngbǎo

是家宅还是城堡

The Royal Residence of the Premier is a colossal building complex; enclosed by a high wall, it looks more like a castle.

family name inherited from one's father. *Ming* is the name given at birth. *Zi* is a courtesy name adopted in adulthood. And a cultured person or an official is likely to assume at least one *hao* or appellation. Chen Tingjing, for example, adopted Wuting Hermit as his appellation. Today, the Chinese name is no longer so complicated, with only the family name and the given name. So the word "name" denotes *xingming* and *mingzi* in Chinese.

绣楼 Xiùlóu
THE EMBROIDERY COMPOUND

"绣" means "embroider" and "绣楼" is a girl's boudoir where she practices embroidery. During the Ming and Qing dynasties, a young lady of an affluent family seldom went out of doors before she got married. She spent every day studying the zither, chess, calligraphy and painting in the Embroidery Compound, to which all her activities were restricted. A number of young ladies lived in the Embroidery Compound of the Premier's Residence. The roof here, unlike those of the adjacent buildings, has no ridge; but it, too, is elegantly shaped. This kind of roof, called a pyramid roof, is often used for buildings of less importance, giving evidence to the girls' low position in both family and society.

One of the girls who lived in the Embroidery Compound, was named Chen Jingyuan, granddaughter of Chen Tingjing. Well educated in such a family, she excelled in poetry and painting. At 17, she got married, but only two years later her husband died. It was generally believed that the family reputation would be marred if a widow remarried, so she returned to her girlhood residence, to live a lonely life until her death.

The Embroidery Compound is an enclosed courtyard with a little garden in which are a pool and a pavilion which commands a good view. This is the entire living space for Chen Jingyuan. All her artistic works on display here, including the poems, paintings and embroidery by this talented girl, seem to articulate her sorrow and loneliness to today's visitors. The bleak compound gnawed away at her youth; before she turned 30, she died of grief, like a tiny star falling onto this little yard.

3

The Birthplace of *The Kangxi Dictionary*

《Kāngxī Zìdiǎn》 de Gùxiāng

《康熙字典》的故乡

To his descendents and the world, Chen Tingjing left a valuable cultural heritage: *The Kangxi Dictionary.*

The residence of the Secretary of the Grand Council

Brick carving on the Screen Wall

Over three centuries ago, Chen Tingjing brought unprecedented prosperity to this residential complex. Meanwhile, he achieved a cultural feat in compiling *The Kangxi Dictionary*, a permanent credit to this residence. *The Kangxi Dictionary* boasted the largest circulation in ancient China. Chen Tingjing was the editor-in-chief of the dictionary and his residence was known as the cradle of *The Kangxi Dictionary*.

By no means was it likely for a small village in a small valley like this to turn out the chief editor for *The Kangxi Dictionary*. But all generations of the Chen family attached importance to education. Whatever the monarchy and whatever the situation, they gave top priority to education. To this end, they built an academy in the outer city, providing a quiet place for the children to study. As a result, the Chen family produced 9 *jinshi* (palace graduates) and 3 members of the Imperial Academy during the Ming and Qing periods. Chen Tingjing was certainly the best of them. More incredibly, when Chen was only 36, his erudition won him the post of Chinese culture tutor to Kangxi, the Manchu emperor. 40 years later when the emperor decided to compile this unprecedented dictionary of Chinese characters, Chen, a learned scholar of excellent character, was the obvious choice for chief editor of this huge project.

A Chinese saying has it that "to accompany the emperor is to keep the tiger company," denoting the potential danger of such a relationship. Both the Ming and Qing regimes employed many people from the Chen family. Chen Tingjing was in company with the emperor for nearly 40 years, establishing a close rapport with Emperor Kangxi; indeed a rare case in Chinese history.

It was difficult for a Chinese official to secure a foothold in the Manchu court unless he was erudite as well as prudent. Although some of Chen Tingjing's ancestors had served the late Ming regime, Chen's academic attainments drew the admiration of Emperor Kangxi. Discreet and courteous, Chen was highly conscientious in the discharge of his duties. He never ganged up with others for personal gains. Despite his remarkable merits, he was not arrogant nor showed off. His lack of political ambition and indifference to fierce competition earned the emperor's trust. During his life, he was promoted 28 times. At

An early edition of *The Kangxi Dictionary*

the age of 66, an age for retirement today, Chen became the Premier, and though Chinese, he was fully trusted by the Manchu emperor. When he turned 73, he was commissioned chief editor of *The Kangxi Dictionary*. The next year witnessed Emperor Kangxi's inspection tour and visit to the Premier's residence. There the emperor was deeply touched by the sight of the white-haired premier working diligently with a group of black-haired scholars. Under such a great strain, Chen died of an illness at 75. Emperor Kangxi lamented Chen's death and referred to him as "a perfect man."

The long-standing prosperity of the Chen family should be attributed to its emphasis on education, superior norms and family tradition. The residence retains its glory thanks to its owner's cultural contribution. Now a Dictionary Museum has been established in the birthplace of *The Kangxi Dictionary*, exhibiting the evolution of Chinese dictionaries.

CHINESE YOU NEED

翰林 hànlín
Member of the Imperial Academy

字典 zìdiǎn
dictionary

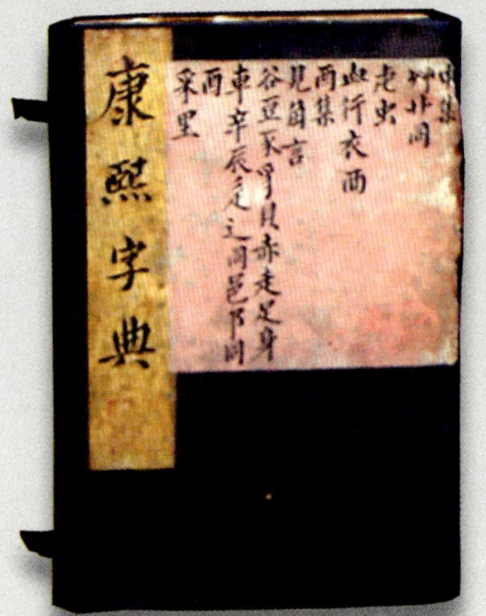

《康熙字典》 «Kāngxī Zìdiǎn»
THE KANGXI DICTIONARY

The Kangxi Dictionary is the first Chinese book with the word "dictionary" in its title. It lasted for six years until the 55th year of the Kangxi Reign (1716). The dictionary contains 47,035 character entries. As a collection of the Chinese characters, *The Kangxi Dictionary* claims many firsts in Chinese lexicographic history: the first dictionary compiled by the government, the only dictionary in honor of a monarch and prefaced by an emperor, the first one with dictionary in its title. For years it remained the largest Chinese dictionary, a record not to be broken until the publication of another dictionary in 1915.

The Kangxi Dictionary is a great work that has stood the test of time. It plays a significant role in the evolution of Chinese characters.

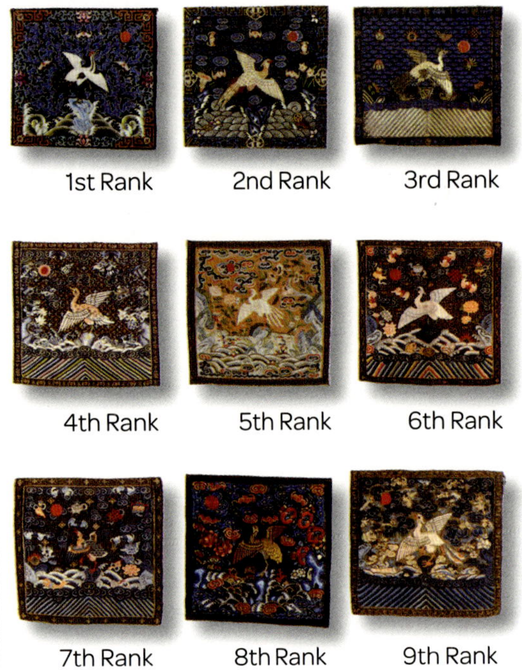

Patch Patterns for Qing Dynasty Officials

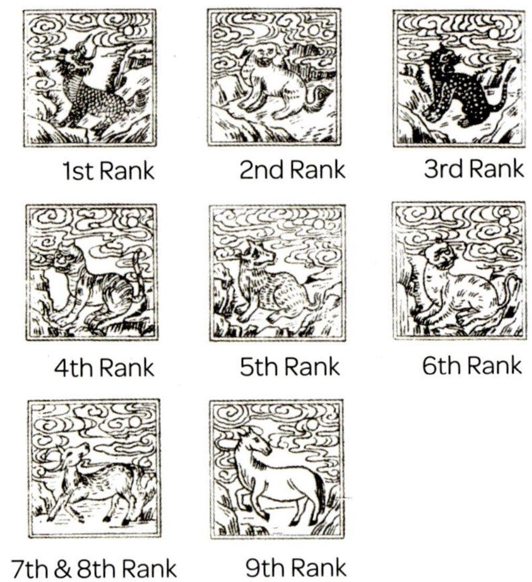

Military Officers' Patches

进士 jìnshì
THE PALACE GRADUATE

From the Sui Dynasty (581-618) to the Qing Dynasty, the Imperial Examination System (科举) determined who could enter the state bureaucracy. The Imperial examinations in the Ming and Qing periods were so strict that all the candidates had to take several exams before they proceeded to the palace examination, which was administered by the emperor himself every three years. A candidate who passed the palace examination would be given the title of *jinshi* ("进士", a palace graduate eligible to serve as an official). Thus, palace graduates were the best scholars selected by the emperor himself.

翰林 hànlín
THE MEMBER OF THE IMPERIAL ACADEMY

Members of the Imperial Academy were officials in ancient China. Although the members assumed different duties in different regimes, they were all erudite scholars. For example, Li Bai, a celebrated Tang poet and Su Shi, a renowned man of letters in the Song Dynasty were both members of the Imperial Academy. In the Ming and Qing periods, all the members were elites selected from among the palace graduates.

皇帝朝服（配康熙像）The Royal Robe

1. 直径半寸的大珍珠帽顶 hat ornamented with a large pearl
2. 红绒 red velvet
3. 披肩领 scarf collar
4. 刺绣金龙 embroidered golden dragon
5. 明黄色长袍 yellow robe
6. 方头黑缎朝靴 square-toed court shoes

官员朝服（配陈廷敬像）The Court Robes

1. 红宝石帽顶 ruby-ornamented hat
2. 红缨 red tassel
3. 108颗圆珠串成的朝珠 court necklace (made of 108 beads)
4. 披肩领 scarf collar
5. 鹤补 crane-patterned patch
6. 石青色长袍 stone-colored robe
7. 黑缎朝靴 black silk court shoes

Since the Manchu established their empire "on horseback", their attire was in keeping to their hunting and nomadic life. The scarf collar and the horse-hoof-shaped cuff are respectively symbolic of the bow and the horse hoof.

清朝官员的服饰

Qīngcháo guānyuán de fúshì

COURT ROBES IN THE QING DYNASTY

1. Official Hat (帽子): The official hat in the Qing Dynasty was ornamented with a jewel on the top. Rank was distinguished by a hierarchy of colors: red, blue, white and yellow. However, the jewels of the same color may symbolize different positions, usually the transparent higher than the opaque. For example, the ruby indicates a higher post than the coral. Since Chen Tingjing was the highest official in the Qing regime, his hat was decorated with a ruby.

2. Court Beads (朝珠): In the Qing Dynasty, only the emperor, the empress dowager, the concubines and high officials were allowed to wear the necklaces called "court beads." The number of the court beads is symbolic of the wearer's rank or status.

3. The Court Robe (官服): The official robe in the Qing Dynasty was a loose garment with a patch (补) on the front. The patch was embroidered with different patterns according to the wearer's rank.

PATCHES FOR QING DYNASTY OFFICIALS

1. Patches for civil officials: crane for the 1st rank, golden pheasant for the 2nd , the peacock for the 3rd, the male wild goose for the 4th, the silver pheasant for the 5th , the egret for the 6th, the mandarin duck for the 7th, the quail for the 8th, the long-tailed fly-catcher for the 9th and the xiezhi (legendary animal credited with the ability to distinguish between right and wrong) for the Chief Censor and the Surveillance Commissioner.

2. Patterned patches for military officers: the kylin (or unicorn, an auspicious legendary animal with a horn and scales all over its body) for the 1st rank, the lion for the 2nd ; the leopard for 3rd, the tiger for the 4th, the bear for the 5th, the young tiger for the 6th; the rhinoceros for the 7th and 8th and the sea horse for the ninth.

4 Historic Huangcheng Village

Bǎinián Huángchéngcūn

百年皇城村

Three centuries ago the ancestor of the village achieved astonishing feats. Today the villagers are pioneering another great cause.

I t has been 300 years since the village reached its zenith. We can't help wondering how the legendary complex has remained intact and why it is so well preserved even today. Haven't the turbulence and wars over the last three centuries faded the memory and glory cherished by the villagers? What are these valley dwellers thinking and what measures have they taken?

Most of the villagers here are descendents of the Chen family. For centuries they have been living in this complex. Self-restrained, they shrouded their eminent ancestor in secrecy. They guarded this huge wealth closely without considering how to make use of it. It was not until 1998 that a man of courage and insight came up with the suggestion that the Premier's Residence be preserved and fully developed. The man who awakened the whole village is none other than Zhang Jiasheng.

Then the village started looking for experts on Chen Tingjing in an effort to do justice to this site of great value. The village committee funded some new houses outside the Premier's Residence. When the villagers moved out of their old houses, extensive renovations began.

The Premier's Residence

Zhiyuan Garden in spring

Between 1998 and 2003, a road leading to the national highway was built, making the hinterland village easily accessible for the first time. Then the village hosted successive seminars; experts on history and culture, groups of people making movies or TV series about the Qing Dynasty, and millions of tourists flocked in. Tourism is a new growth industry in the village. In 2003, Huangcheng Xiangfu Group was founded. Zhang Jiasheng, the first man to advocate development, was the chairman of the board. Within the Goup there is an important branch called Department of Cultural Studies. Probably Cheng Tingjing realized three centuries ago that the latent zest and respect for culture would one day pulsate again in the veins of his descendants.

Inside of Dianhantang

Three centuries ago the village in this valley produced an outstanding scholar and statesman. Today his descendants have inherited his intelligence, courage and strong belief in education. Undoubtedly, the Premier's Residence will remain lofty and majestic in this valley, a testimony to the ancestor's glory and the descendants' enterprising spirit.

CHINESE YOU NEED

旅游业 lǚyóuyè
the tourism industry

HEAVENLY HUIZHOU

Táohuāyuán Lǐ de Rénjiā — Huīzhōu Yìnxiàng

桃花源里的人家——徽州印象

By Hua Sha, Chu Dandan
Photographs by Zhang Hengquan, Mao Yaoquan, Zhu Jiang, Tang Zuhuai
Translated by Wei Lingcha, Duan Suping

In south-eastern China, there is a place traditionally known as Huizhou. It is a place of natural beauty. A visit to a local house is always a surprise sojourn: in contrast to its relatively humble exterior, each house's interior is exceedingly extravagant. Of all Huizhou structures, the most typical ones are the ancestral halls and honorific archways which are symbols of family honor and eternal tribute to traditional local values. Despite their expertise in business, people in Huizhou prefer to live a simple and unpretentious life. Living in the old houses inherited from their forbearers, they strive quietly for excellent preservation of their ancient culture.

SECTIONS:

1. Black Tiles and White Walls
2. Fortunes Spent
3. Memorial Arch: A Stone Award
4. Living History Along the Ancient Street

1 Black Tiles and White Walls

Qīngwǎ Báiqiáng — Huà Lǐ Rénjiā

青瓦白墙——画里人家

About 1,600 years ago, a Chinese poet wrote about a place called "Peach Blossom Land." It is enclosed by mountains and noted for its scenic beauty. Free of wars and immune to the change of dynasties, people there work peacefully and live a carefree life. One generation goes and another comes, but lasting joy and harmony reign supreme. Thus the Peach Blossom Land has become a dreamland for generations of Chinese. Should such a land exist, it would be a "living museum" of Chinese culture, it presents not only fabulous and unique scenery but also traditional values and lifestyle.

In the early morning, when the first rays of sunshine disperse the mist in a mountain cove, a valley unfolds with golden rape blossoms blooming all over the nearby hills and dales. Wisps of smoke rise from the village chimneys. In twos and threes, the villagers leave their houses, with either a hoe on the shoulder or two bamboo baskets on a shoulder pole. New day has begun.

Called Hucun, the little village nestles peacefully between mountains and a river. Similar villages abound in Huizhou. Compared to the blue sky, green mountains and golden flowers, the houses appear extraordinarily modest and elegant in color. All the houses here are black-and-white. White and high, the walls are free of any color decoration. All the roofs and wall tops are covered with black tiles. Like black eyes set off against a white complexion, they form a perfect combination.

The high exterior walls are called *matou* (literally horse's head). Turning upward, the ridge on the walls is the only type of decoration that can be seen from the outside. In the past, men in Huizhou were perennially out on business, leaving their wives alone at home. Thus high walls were built to prevent theft and fire and to protect privacy. The lanes between houses are narrow and long, stretching as far as the eye can see. A walk along the lane is like a journey across an ancient Chinese ink-wash painting.

Mr. Zhang, a local native over 70 years old, is very familiar with the history of the village. There are only two original clans in the village: Hu and Zhang. Later, others moved in. Thanks to its good *fengshui* *, the village's population flourished. The ancestors of the villagers mostly made their fortunes in commerce and then built large houses. At present, the villagers are engaged mainly in sericulture. Many of their children have left the village for university while the elders rear silkworms and reel off raw silk from cocoons at home. They live comfortably. Pointing at his sister, Mr. Zhang said, "This is my elder sister. Although she is 91 years old, she is neither hard of hearing nor dim-sighted. The other day she even flew to Shenzhen to visit her granddaughter."

Thanks, perhaps, to this blessed sacred land, the village boasts more than 20 people who are nearly 100 years old, among less than 1,000 villagers. Generation after generation, they have lived in their ancestral houses, as if never affected by the "winds and storms" outside. Like the 1,000-year-old tree at the entrance to the village that has been watching the flowers bloom and wither with the flow of time, the villagers continue to live and thrive here.

CHINESE YOU NEED

青瓦 qīngwǎ
black tiles

白墙 báiqiáng
white walls

朴素 pǔsù
simplicity

Fengshui: traditional Chinese practice of determining the location of a house, tomb, etc., thought to have a vital bearing on the fortune of the owner, user, etc.

Ancient bridge in Lihu Village

Horse head-shaped walls

Villagers walking on a bamboo bridge

Golden rape blossoms

Mr. Zhang and his elder sister

2 Fortunes Spent

Háozhái yǔ Cítáng — Cáifù de Zhōngdiǎn

豪宅与祠堂——财富的终点

Once the most famous merchants in China, the owners of these Huizhou residences spent their entire fortunes on their mansions.

Here people live peaceful lives in their traditional houses.

The Huizhou residence, covered with black tiles and enclosed by white walls, appears simple and humble, though the interior is exquisitely decorated. The beams, door leaves, eaves, bricks and tiles are all ornamented with exquisite carvings. Each piece is a fine work of art. While gasping with admiration at the gorgeous adornment in a house, we could not help wondering: Who the owner was? Why did he spend a fortune on a residence with such luxurious interior ornaments and such a deliberately unassuming exterior?

This house is called Chengzhi Hall. Its owner was a salt dealer named Wang Dinggui. It is said that this structure cost him 600,000 *liang* of silver. Apart from that, he also spent 100 *liang* of gold on the gold foil covering the beams and pillars, which still look rich and splendid today. Even the inconspicuous step board in front of the bed and the corner braces under the beams are also finely carved and embellished with gold or jade. On the main beam in the front hall is a wood carving, one meter long and 20 centimeters wide, depicting boys celebrating the Lantern Festival which marks the end of Chinese New Year celebrations. They beat drums, clang gongs, and perform the lion or the dragon dance. Distinctive from each other, every figure is vividly characterized. This scene is called "One Hundred Boys Celebrating the Lantern Festival," a conventional token of the owner's wish for many descendents.

There are countless extravagant mansions in Huizhou. They were built by the richest merchants in China, who shared the same title: Hui Merchants.

In fact, Huizhou men had no choice but to turn to commerce for a living, because their land was barren, and, agriculture, unproductive. Normally, teenage boys here had to travel to big cities like Hangzhou and Yangzhou

to work as apprentices in trade and commerce. They mainly engaged in the salt, pawning, tea and timber industries. Education was so highly valued in Huizhou that people there never gave up study wherever they went. Their skill in trading also helped them become leaders in their guilds. As early as the Song Dynasty (960-1279), the Hui merchants had already evolved into the largest group of their kind in China. They journeyed across China and their business reached as far as Japan and Southeast Asia. During that time, Huizhou tea became the favorite luxury item of the British aristocracy.

It was Huizhou merchants who, generation after generation, accumulated large fortunes and then spent them on the land of Huizhou.

An old saying has it that "If you make a fortune without returning home, you are like a man walking at night in fancy clothing-you will remain obscure." The Hui merchant, who went to a strange land in his teenage years, left his native place only to return in glory. With the profits from his business, he would not consider investment in a larger business. His wish was to return home and glorify his ancestors by buying a piece of land and building a grand house.

More typical of the Hui people's concept of wealth is having a "*tianjing*," a tiny square courtyard in each house. The high walls ensure safety but fail to provide sufficient light. It is the quadrangle that fills the rooms around with light. A Japanese architect once offered this description of Huizhou's "*tianjing*": "the interior space is flooded with quiet illumination from above. People seem to have faded away here. Looking up from the yard, one sees a rectangle vista framed with eaves. Secluded tranquility reigns."

Quadrangle

Interior of a Hui residence

Grocery baskets

3

Memorial Arch: A Stone Award

Páifāng — Zhuānshí de "Jiǎngzhuàng"

牌坊——砖石的"奖状"

The memorial arch, a structure like a gate, can be found everywhere in the countryside of Huizhou. It is a symbol of honor. The greatest honor for a person is the construction of a memorial arch bearing his or her name. However, money was not the only prerequisite for building a memorial arch. A memorial arch, usually in recognition of a certain person or deed, could only be built with the emperor or the clan's approval. More than a letter or notice of commendation, the memorial arch perpetuated the glory bestowed upon the family.

Of the traditional Chinese values, four are most prized: loyalty, filial piety, chastity, and righteousness. Loyalty emphasizes devotion to one's master or nation. Filial piety involves obedience to one's parents. A woman's quality of being faithful to her husband is called chastity. Righteousness indicates that one is willing to give all for fraternity or friendship. There are over 1,000 memorial arches of various sizes in Huizhou. Those in commendation of loyalty and righteousness were erected by imperial order. Hence they were splendid and gorgeous. The most common arches here were those in honor of female chastity.

Conventionally a man in Huizhou was supposed to leave home on business at 16, so he had to get married at 13 or 14. Out on business, he would not return home for several years—dozen or even dozens. The wife, throughout her life, could spend merely a few years with her husband. Indeed, behind the chastity archways were numerous lonely hearts shedding bitter tears.

CHINESE YOU NEED

牌坊 páifāng
memorial Arch

节 jié
chastity

忠 zhōng
loyalty

义 yì
righteousness

孝 xiào
filial piety

4

Living History Along the Ancient Street

Lǎojiē — Huózhe de Lìshǐ

老街——活着的历史

Huizhou is a living cultural museum. Every effort has been made to preserve the tradition in Huizhou.

可口可乐
酒楼
缅甸玉器专卖
经营范围：翡玉挂件 手镯

Huizhou: an ink-wash painting comes to life

True to its name, Old Street is ancient. Since the Song Dynasty, it has been a street with brisk business. Miraculously, it seems the street has remained almost exactly the same after so many centuries. The long-worn brown stone plates are shining. The scent of herbs pervades the traditional Chinese pharmacies. The female silk thread reelers are transforming fresh cocoons into white quilts. And a peddler, carrying his tiny kitchen on a pole, is hawking his wonton. Thus unfurls a beautiful, old Chinese painting.

Many are wondering how the ancient look has been so well preserved throughout history. Perhaps we can find the answers from a few locals.

Mr. Zhu, a native of Huizhou, used to study ancient architecture. He traveled to many villages in Huizhou and collected a lot of antiques from ancient houses: carvings, pillars, beams, doors, windows, stone seats, etc. He spent seven years and all his savings, with the support of his entire family, and built up a garden to house all the antiques he had collected. Surrounded by streams and hills, the garden, named The Purple Garden, is near the county town.

Shao Maoshen is in his eighties. He has long retired from his teaching post at the primary school in Fuling village. Popular here is a folk performance called Lion Dance. Every child has to learn it. Over the past two centuries, the lion dance has been performed at the village fair in the first lunar month, usually lasting four days beginning on the 14th. However, nowadays most young villagers leave the village to study or work, and there are fewer and fewer lion dance learners. Mr. Zhong, who has been fond of the lion dance

since his childhood, was afraid that this valuable art would be lost. So he spent three years writing a book titled *The Lion Dance in Fuling* and had it published at his own expense. The book was the fruit of his painstaking efforts. With it in his hands, the octogenarian was very proud: "After all it is a legacy for our descendants."

It is the ordinary people in Huizhou who have protected their land. Indifferent to fame or fortune, they quietly and unswervingly protect their homes as well as their ancestors' legacy, tangible and intangible.

CHINESE YOU NEED

活的历史 huó de lìshǐ
living history

老街 lǎojiē
ancient street

图书在版编目(CIP)数据

中国文化档案＝Cultural Files：Cultural Relics. 人文景观/《汉语世界》杂志社编. —北京：商务印书馆，2011
ISBN 978-7-100-07400-1

Ⅰ.①中… Ⅱ.①汉… Ⅲ.①名胜古迹—简介—中国 Ⅳ.①K928.7

中国版本图书馆CIP数据核字(2010)第188418号

中国文化档案：人文景观

《汉语世界》杂志社　编

商务印书馆出版
(北京王府井大街36号　邮政编码 100710)
商务印书馆发行
北京瑞古冠中印刷厂印刷
ISBN 978-7-100-07400-1

2011年4月第1版　开本889×1194　1/16
2011年4月北京第1次印刷　印张7¼
定价：89.00元